THE ESSENCE OF ENGLISH LIFE

The Essence of

English Life

SHEILA PICKLES

PHOTOGRAPHS BY ROSEMARY WELLER

HARMONY BOOKS
NEW YORK

For Janet

Published by Harmony Books,
a division of Crown Publishers, Inc.,
201 East 50th Street, New York, New York 10022.
Member of the Crown Publishing Group.
Random House, Inc. New York, Toronto, London, Sydney, Auckland.
Published in Great Britain by Pavilion Books in 1993.

Harmony and colophon are trademarks of
Crown Publishers, Inc.

Manufactured in Hong Kong by Imago
ISBN: 0–517–59280–0
10 9 8 7 6 5 4 3 2 1

Library of Congress Cataloging-in-Publication Data
Pickles, Sheila.
The essence of English life/Sheila Pickles – – 1st ed.
p.   cm.
"First published in Great Britain in 1993 by Pavilion Books
Limited" – – T.p. verso.
ISBN 0–517–59280–0 : $20.00
1. National characteristics, English. 2. England – – Social life and
customs. 3. England – – Literary collections. I. Title.
DA118.P53   1983
942 – dc20   93 – 18044
CIP

First American Edition

C o n t e n t s

Introduction

I GREW up in the Yorkshire countryside in the decade immediately following the Second World War. It seems to me in retrospect that during this period we were lulled into a false sense of security as the country recovered from the war. For my sister, Susan, and me it was an age when Nanny knew best and we were forbidden to eat in the street. There was also less questioning of values, more respect between men, and we were certainly proud to be British. Several decades later, life is quite different; giant strides are being made in technology, but at the same time I rejoice that so many of our unique customs are being upheld.

I was born in Heptonstall, an ancient weaving village perched high on the edge of the moors, and when I was seven we moved to Carr House, my mother's family home in the country outside Hebden Bridge where her family had lived for several generations. I would set off after breakfast on my new bicycle and cycle up Cragg Vale on to the Pennine moors, returning only in time for lunch — something no mother would encourage even a fifteen-year-old to do today. Perhaps it was the naïvety of youth, but it seems to me that life at that time had a leisurely pace and an innocence which has long been lost.

My children, James, aged ten, and Charlotte Rose, nine, are growing up in London, and my husband, David, and I have tried to provide similar surroundings to those I so enjoyed as a child. We were lucky to find a Georgian house in Canonbury, built in 1780, which has the scale of a country house, and the advantage of a large garden, perfect for tree climbing, ball games and pets.

I write this at a time when the future of England is in the balance. Britain has chosen to become part of a closer Europe, and while there are good reasons for European integration, both practical and idealistic, it will also inevitably lead to some loss of individuality and identity. I already mourn the loss of the sovereign, the guinea and our eccentric threepenny bit, and I resent decimalization. My children do not know what 'Sing a song of sixpence' means, and although I appreciate that standardization makes life easier for the computer operator, I question whether it adds any quality to our lives.

> Old customs! Oh! I love the sound
> However simple they may be:
> Whate'er with time hath sanction found,
> Is welcome and is dear to me.
> Pride grows above simplicity,
> And spurns them from her haughty mind,
> And soon the poet's song will be
> The only refuge they can find.
>
> JOHN CLARE

These stirring lines by John Clare perfectly encapsulate my own feelings about tradition. Clare also had a deep love for the English countryside, and expressed it so perfectly, which is why I have used extracts from 'The Shepherd's Calendar' to introduce each season.

In this book I have tried to capture what is precious and typical in English life, namely those characteristic customs and events that mean so much: some from the past, some from today, but all personal to me. The rhythm of our year is dictated by the seasons, and has altered little since the early nineteenth century, when John Clare was writing his poetry. The structure of English life is still based today on the church calendar as it has been for centuries. Some of the traditions may be found elsewhere, but it is the part they play in the life of the rural community throughout the year which makes them quintessentially English.

Sheila Pickles
Old House, Canonbury, 1993

S P R I N G

Sweet month! thy pleasures bid thee be
The fairest child of spring;
And every hour, that comes with thee,
Comes some raw joy to bring:
The trees still deepen in their bloom,
Grass greens the meadow lands,
And flowers with every morning come,
As dropt by fairy hands.

JOHN CLARE

ALTHOUGH the calendar year begins and ends in midwinter, we tend to think of spring as the first season of the year, and warmly welcome its first signs and coaxing sunlight. The spring equinox is the third week in March, but the arrival of spring varies in different parts of the country and comes at a different time each year, lending it a certain unpredictability. No other season is awaited with such anticipation, and the change, when it does come, is dramatic. One day the ground is hard and the landscape bleak, and then after a few hours of sunshine leaf-buds are opening and small shoots are starting to appear. This indication that Nature has been hard at work through the cruel winter months to bring us new life is symbolic; this is the time to rejoice that winter has been defeated, spring is here at last, and the annual pageant of the seasons is already unfolding once again.

The snowdrop is the first sign of spring, even if snow has often fallen long after the green spears have pushed their way up through the frozen ground. By mid February, small clumps of crocus start to appear and, if the winter has been mild, dog violets can be found between the York stone flags. Daffodils and narcissi may be seen nodding their heads in the border in the March wind, and blue and white aconites flower under the bare branches of the tree peony, whose large leaves will later shade the ground.

The pleasure of a garden in spring lies in the variety of colour available, which can make it look like a giant tapestry. It is the only moment of the year when I blend all the colours in together — drifts of yellow and purple crocus, blue dwarf iris, yellow tulips growing up through pale blue forget-me-nots. Orange is not one of my favourite colours, but having seen Vita Sackville-West's cottage garden at Sissinghurst, full of red, orange and yellow flowers in midsummer, I decided to have a corner in these colours just for the spring. I have planted tall crown imperials behind red and yellow tulips, with miniature yellow daffodils growing through yellow alyssum ground cover. Wallflowers planted in pots in the autumn soon provide an early show of colour and a delicious scent, while spears of lily of the valley will soon be visible underneath the giant camellia. This has been in bud now since the autumn and will provide beautiful sprays of flowers for the dining table all through spring.

The First Delicate Buds

IT has been said that in the spring a young man's fancy turns to thoughts of love, whereas a married man thinks only of the jobs which are waiting to be done. Nowhere could this be truer than in the garden. No matter how well we put the garden to bed before the winter, there is always a lot to be done once the bad weather finally ends and we can get outside.

Most spring flowers have a good scent, but my favourite is a white daphne which I brought with me to my London garden and planted near the house so that we would have the benefit of its sweet scent in early spring. I am not particularly fond of mahonia as a plant, but having inherited one in the garden I have grown to appreciate it. It is old and very large. Being evergreen it retains its shape and leaves all year round, which are stacked behind it. More importantly, it has a powerful scent, and just one spray of it, cut and put in a vase, will make the whole room smell of lily of the valley.

By March the small white stars of the magnolia stellata are starting to come out, and the garden bed between the large plane trees planted with euphorbias, hellebores, hostas and primroses is at its best. Even when there are few flowers in bloom,

their shapes are so pleasing and well defined that they lend a grace and a peaceful quality to the garden. There are two plants that I grow partly with the house in mind. Solomon's seal grows well under the trees, and looks wonderful when the arched stems with their hanging green-tipped bells are cut and brought indoors. In late spring, dicentra spectabilis, or Love Lies Bleeding, comes out, and I am so fond of this pretty romantic plant, with its elegant arching sprays of tiny pink hanging hearts, that I grow the pink and white varieties side by side.

Spring is the time when the gardener needs to put on his gardening gloves and take secateurs in hand, for there is much pruning to be done and many plants to be fed and fertilized. It is also time to start thinking about sowing annuals: snapdragons, tobacco plants, rudbeckia, cosmeas, clarkia, larkspur — all the plants which will make a good show in the herbaceous border later in the year. The lawn too is beginning to need attention, although I always ask David to delay mowing it for the first time, for I so love to see it covered in daisies. I often ask myself who it was who decided which are the plants and which the weeds . . .

St Valentine's Day

ST Valentine's Day has recently been omitted from the calendar of saints' days, as the Church claims that it is unable to prove his existence. However, he has remained the most popular of saints, and 14 February the most familiar of dates, for this is the day on which sweethearts exchange tokens of their affection in the form of flowers, cards and romantic gifts.

> Last Valentine, the day when birds of kind
> Their paramours with mutual chirpings find
> I early rose just at the break of day,
> Before the sun had chased the stars away:
> A-field I went, amid the morning dew,
> To milk my kine (for so should housewives do)
> Thee first I spied — and the first swain we see,
> In spite of Fortune shall our true love be.
>
> JOHN GAY

In this verse Gay is referring to the seventeenth-century belief that one was destined to marry the first unmarried person whom one met on St Valentine's morning. We think of this day as an opportunity for a shy admirer to reveal his hand, and true romantics may be disappointed to know that the original ceremony of St Valentine's Day was a type of lottery. In medieval times, on the evening of 13 February, village lads and lasses would gather together and draw lots to find their valentine, on whom they lavished attention for several days. Such little sport often ended in love — and even more often, one imagines, in outrage or hilarity.

The Victorians celebrated St Valentine's Day with embroidered hearts and intricate cards, many of which they made themselves and in which they wrote their own verses. In the last century, too, the language of flowers became extremely popular; suitors sent red roses to signify their love, or perhaps white lilac in the first throes of romance.

Today the custom continues and keepsakes are given. Whether the gifts are a simple posy or a silver locket is immaterial, for it is the thought that counts, and this day above all others provides the chance to say 'I love you'.

The Great English Breakfast

IN the spring, after months spent mostly indoors, I always have an urge to get outside and go on an outing. Whether it is a day out in the country, an overnight stay at a bed and breakfast farmhouse, a country inn or a country house hotel, the day starts with the great English breakfast. This usually means eggs — poached eggs, scrambled eggs or fried eggs — served with rashers of bacon, tomatoes, sausages and large field mushrooms. A northern favourite is black pudding — thick slices of dark sausage meat served on fried bread — a good start to the day. Children might have just a soft boiled egg with 'soldiers' — strips of buttered toast which they love to dip into the runny yolk. When I first went to school eggs were rationed and a rare treat. Instead we were served bacon or dripping — the hot bacon fat into which we dipped our bread. Very often breakfast will have been cooked on an Aga, the famous cooker invented by Dr Aga, a Swede, at the turn of the century. Coming downstairs on a cold morning to a kitchen warmed by an Aga is one of the most comforting things I know.

The radio programme *The Archers*, 'an everyday story of country folk', is part of my daily routine, and even when I am city bound I enjoy hearing about the farming community of fictional Ambridge. This is a good time to be on a farm, for the lambing starts in the spring and many is the time I have seen a farmer's wife feeding a lamb with a baby's bottle. Small boys like William and the Outlaws are off with jam jars to catch frogspawn, and wild ducks have started to look for places to make a nest and lay their eggs.

One of the great pleasures of being in the country is the pub lunch. Sitting outside in the fresh air with a glass of beer, shandy or cider and a ploughman's lunch of bread and cheese is a welcome break. Many public houses have been there for centuries, some of them originally coaching inns where travellers stopped to change their horses. Today they play an important part in the country, for the church and the pub are the centre of village life.

Shrove Tuesday and Mothering Sunday

I'll to thee a simnel bring
'Gainst thou go a-mothering;
So that, when she blesses thee
Half that blessing thou'lt give me.

ROBERT HERRICK

SOON after St Valentine's Day comes Ash Wednesday, marking the beginning of Lent. Traditionally a period of fasting, Lent lasts for forty days and ends on Easter Sunday. The day before Ash Wednesday is known as Shrove Tuesday, and was a day of confession before Lent. We know it as Pancake Day, and this is because in earlier, stricter times dairy products and eggs were forbidden in Lent so all those remaining in the larder were made into pancakes and eaten up before the fast began.

Our pancakes are served at the end of the meal and have sugar and lemon juice sprinkled over them before they are rolled up. The children all have a go at tossing them in the air from the flat-bottomed pan, and there is much delight when they stick on the ceiling.

On Midlent Sunday, traditionally three Sundays before Easter, girls in service in Victorian times were allowed to 'go a-mothering' — that is to say, home to see their mothers — and the day came to be called Mothering Sunday. One can imagine how the mother looked forward to it, having sent her child off at twelve or fourteen to work in a grand household and perhaps having only seen

PANCAKES

4 oz/120g/8 tbsp plain white flour
Large pinch of salt
1 egg
1/2 pint of milk
1 tbsp melted butter

Sift the flour and salt into a bowl. Beat to smooth creamy batter with unbeaten egg, half the milk and melted butter. Stir in remaining milk. Leave to stand for an hour in a cool place. Lightly brush the base of the frying pan with melted butter and stand over medium heat. When pan and butter are hot, pour in two or three tablespoonfuls of batter (enough to coat the base of the pan thinly). Fry until golden brown, turn over by tossing in the air. Cook the second side until golden and mottled. Remove and repeat with the rest of batter. Makes eight pancakes.

her on this one day of the year ever since. Some daughters would have made a simnel cake (see *Easter* for the recipe) or brought a small trinket; more often than not they would have picked a bunch of violets on the way home.

Today most English children still enjoy celebrating Mothering Sunday, or Mother's Day, and happily the tradition continues with hand-made cards and presents as well as the commercial kind.

Easter

EASTER has always been a moveable feast in the Church calendar. On the Thursday before Easter, known as Maundy Thursday, the Queen gives out Maundy money to the poor. This 600-year-old custom is a gesture of humility, recalling Jesus washing the apostles' feet. On the following day, Good Friday, we eat Hot Cross Buns, which have the symbolic cross on the top.

In the Calder Valley, in Yorkshire, Good Friday has a double significance, for it is also Pace Egging Day. The local schools re-enact the age-old play of St George and the Dragon. This is spoken in thick Yorkshire dialect and takes place in the street.

When the play was over, we used to go into the fields with large brown paper carrier bags, to collect the small dock leaves (*Polygonum bistorta*) which grow only around Hebden Bridge and Mytholmroyd, for which we were rewarded by our parents with sixpence a bag. These were taken home, cooked with spring onions, baby nettles and oatmeal, and made into the most delicious supper dish imaginable. No one remembers the origins of the dish, but during the Second World War the propaganda broadcaster Lord Haw Haw told the Germans that Dock Pudding was being made and announced that the food shortage in Yorkshire was so bad that the people were reduced to eating grass.

All over the country on Easter Sunday morning Easter eggs are given as a symbol of new life. In addition to chocolate eggs, many hen's eggs will have been hand-painted by children, and in some places dummy eggs are rolled down hills or Easter egg hunts are arranged. However, no Yorkshire woman would let Easter Sunday go by without serving a Simnel Cake. This deep round fruit cake, covered in marzipan and decorated on top with a circle of marzipan balls, was the invention of Lambert Simnel. He was a pretender to the throne who claimed to be one of the Princes in the Tower. When he was caught, he had a stroke of luck, for King Henry VII learned that he was a good cook, his father being a baker, and instead of beheading him, which was the usual punishment for treason, Henry set him to work in the Palace kitchen.

I am also a great believer in eating the food traditionally associated

SIMNEL CAKE

3 oz / 90g / 6 tbsp butter
3 oz / 90g / 6 tbsp sugar
2 eggs
3 oz / 90g / 6 tbsp plain flour
1 oz / 130g / 2 tbsp ground rice or rice flour
6 oz / 180g / 7/8 cup currants
A pinch of cinnamon and nutmeg
Grated rind of a lemon
1 tsp lemon juice

Almond Paste

5 oz / 150g / 1¼ cups ground almonds
5 oz / 150g / 1¼ cups caster sugar
Few drops of almond essence
1 egg

Rub almonds and sugar together in a bowl by hand. Add almond essence and ⅔ of the beaten egg. It should be easy to handle as half the paste is used as a layer in the centre of the cake and the other half has to be rolled into balls to decorate the top.

Put half the cake mixture into the bottom of a deep, 7½" diameter cake tin, and cover with a layer of almond paste. Fill the tin with the remaining mixture and bake in centre of a moderate oven (375°F/190°C/Gas 5, reduced to 325°F/170°C/Gas 3 after 20 minutes) for 1—1¼ hours. When the cake is almost baked, place almond paste balls round the top of the cake. Brush over with beaten egg and cook for a further ten minutes.

with specific seasons on account of the availability of the ingredients and the climate. Thus I look forward to salmon and strawberries in the summer, game in the autumn, and oysters when there is an 'r' in the month. Nowadays, of course, many foods are available practically all the year round, thanks to advances in food preservation and wider distribution, but just as I dislike daffodils before Christmas and chrysanthemums in June, so I believe that whenever possible food should be eaten fresh and in season. Indeed, each Saint's Day can be celebrated with the appropriate dish.

Bluebells

ON 23 April you can see flags flying all over England, for not only is it St George's Day, but also Shakespeare's birthday. Our national flag, the Union Jack, is made up of the red cross of St George, the patron saint of England, the white saltire, or diagonal cross, of St Andrew, the patron saint of Scotland, surmounted by the red saltire of St Patrick, the patron saint of Ireland, against the blue ground of the banner of St Andrew. The colours are proudly carried by the Girl Guides as they march to church in their blue blouses to show their respect to their company and their town.

In the hedgerows the hawthorn has opened her lime-green buds, and village children nibble it as they walk to school. Its country nickname is bread and butter, and country people know that once the hawthorn is out, the spring flowers will soon follow. The pussy willow will put out her furry blooms down by the brook, and banks of Lent lilies will lend colour to the landscape. Man cannot improve on nature in the spring, and I often feel that the native flora of the countryside is preferable to that which has been introduced from elsewhere. The Tai Haku cherry tree in my garden with its snow white blossom is exotic and very pretty, and I am fond too of my magnolia soulangeana with its scented white cups which open on naked branches; but neither of them can compare with the carpet of bluebells to be found in the woods, or meadows of snakeshead fritillaries. The wild flowers of spring have a pure and simple beauty about them which makes the English countryside quite unique.

Stories in the Nursery

FOR me, one of the pleasures of having children was in rediscovering the books I had enjoyed as a child. I still get intense pleasure from reading A. A. Milne's *When We Were Very Young* and *Now We Are Six* from very old, thin, blue, mildewed copies, printed in the 1930s. Beatrix Potter's Jemima Puddle-Duck, Mr Jeremy Fisher and Peter Rabbit are loved as greatly by my children as they were by me. I have always thought how wise Beatrix Potter was to insist that her publisher print her stories in such tiny books, for children have tiny hands and love to be able to hold the books themselves — all the better to disapprove of the cunning of the fox in poor *Jemima Puddle-Duck*, the selfishness of the Two Bad Mice and the naughty Miss Moppet teasing the mouse. 'No mouse' were the first two words my daughter, Charlotte Rose, ever put together, as I read one day how Miss Moppet untied the duster and found nothing inside.

We feared for Mole in the wild wood in *The Wind in the Willows*, and laughed at the foolish, adventure-loving Toad with his garage full of crashed cars. Like J. M. Barrie's *Peter Pan*, Lewis Carroll's *Alice in Wonderland* and *Through the Looking Glass* have intrigued children and grown-ups alike. These Victorian children's stories can be read and analysed on several levels. As a child I was able to relate to Richmal Crompton's character William. Her books perfectly captured middle-class life in an English village as I remember it. My schoolfriends and I read our way through series after series of Enid Blyton and were gently led on to E. Nesbit, Noel Streatfeild and C. S. Lewis. Years later I find them very comforting to read — old friends, undemanding and familiar. Many of them are available today on tape and video, both of which have their place, but there is nothing like sitting on a mother's lap and starting a new story.

Porcelain and Pottery

AREAS of prosperity in England have always tended to be clustered near to natural resources and the manufacturing industries which depend on them. The cotton industry in Lancashire grew up because the climate there was so damp that the thread did not break. The Sheffield steel industry, shipbuilding on the Tyne, and the coal mines of the Black Country all contributed to the great wealth of England in Queen Victoria's day. Perhaps it is because I have so enjoyed the novels of Arnold Bennett, such as *Anna of the Five Towns*, that I have always been particularly fond of the Potteries in Staffordshire. This district in fact contains numerous small industrial towns which have been the centre for the manufacture of porcelain and pottery for centuries. I remember being told as a child how to tell the difference between the two. Porcelain, or china, differs from ordinary pottery in being semi-transparent: if you hold a china cup up to the light you can see your fingers through it. This is because it is made from fine white clay mixed with powdered bone — hence 'bone china'. In the Middle Ages only the Chinese had perfected the art of making porcelain, and as a result a piece of 'china' was a gift fit for a king. It is very easy to tell if you are dining with someone who lives in the Potteries region, for if they do not recognize the pattern of china from which they are eating they will immediately pick it up and look underneath to see who made it. A friend of mine was at a dinner party when a short-sighted guest picked up her soup plate, having not recognized the pattern, and turned it over — only to discover that she had not recognized it because the bowl was full of soup.

A complete dinner service is a wonderful thing to have, and the quantity of tureens, meat platters, vegetable dishes, sauce boats and ladles tells us much about how people used to eat and present their food a century ago. The most traditional dinner service is probably Spode's Willow Pattern, although for grand dining there is nothing to beat Old Imari by Royal Grand Derby. If I had to select just one, however, it would have to be Asiatic Pheasant: the pale lavender blue bird on the white background is never out of place.

SUMMER

Now summer is in flower, and Nature's hum
Is never silent round her bounteous bloom;
Insects, as small as dust, have never done
With glitt'ring dance, and reeling in the sun;
And green wood-fly, and blossom-haunting bee,
Are never weary of their melody.
Round field and hedge, flowers in full glory twine,
Large bindweed bells, wild hop, and streak'd woodbine,
That lift athirst their slender-throated flowers,
Agape for dew-falls, and for honey showers;
These o'er each bush in sweet disorder run,
And spread their wild hues to the sultry sun.

JOHN CLARE

For many English people the essence of summer is 'the Season'. Long gone are the days when country aristocrats took a house in London for the Season in order to present their daughter at Court and find a suitable husband for her. However, most of the events associated with it, many of them sporting ones, live on as entertainments to which people go with their friends or to entertain their business associates. Some of the events, such as polo at Windsor, used to be accessible only to the upper classes; now, however, almost all the occasions which make up the English Season are open to everybody.

Opening the Season is the Oxford and Cambridge Boat Race, the annual rowing contest between the crews of our great Universities. It actually takes place in April on the four mile stretch of the Thames between Putney and Mortlake, and supporters line the banks of the river and cheer the eights on to victory. A small flotilla follows the Blue boats, and millions more watch the race on television.

On the Queen's official birthday in June the ceremony of Trooping the Colour is held, when she inspects the troops of the seven regiments which make up her Household Division. It is an elaborate ceremony peculiar to the British and while it may seem like playing at soldiers, it symbolizes the Army's allegiance to the Crown. At eleven o'clock, on arrival at Horse Guards Parade, the Queen salutes her mother, takes the royal salute for her official birthday and then inspects the Guard of Honour. This is followed by a march past, while the band plays popular tunes and regimental marches. At the end of the ceremony she returns to Buckingham Palace to take her place on the balcony with other members of the Royal Family to see the RAF flypast.

Most members of 'the royal firm', as they sometimes refer to themselves, attend some part of the Season. Princess Anne regularly rides at the Badminton Horse Trials in Gloucestershire, and Prince Charles enjoys competing in polo matches. The Queen and her mother, Queen Elizabeth The Queen Mother, often have horses running at The Grand National, the great steeplechase which takes place at Aintree, or the Derby, probably the most popular sporting event of the Season. The most fashionable, certainly the most fashion-conscious, is Royal Ascot when punters dress up in their finery, the gentlemen sporting top hats and tails. It is fun to view the horses, note who is riding and then place a bet with a bookmaker. My father always enjoyed race-meetings and taught me to place all my money for betting in one pocket and my winnings in another and never to mix the two. I rarely come away at the end of the day with any money in hand, but it is fun to have a flutter, and you cannot expect much success if, like me, you base your choice on the name of the horse.

Bounteous Bloom

IN medieval and Tudor England, May Day was a public holiday and working folk were up with the dawn to go a-Maying in the woods. Branches of hawthorn trees and flowers were gathered and borne back in triumph to the villages, to the accompaniment of music and dancing. This was known as 'bringing home the May'. The fairest maid of the village was crowned Queen of the May, and the centre of the festivities was the Maypole which was decorated with ribbons, garlands and wreaths. Around it the lads and lasses leaped and sang and there was much merry-making. The local gentry used to come out of their great houses and join in the fun, and it was a day of celebration for all. This annual custom was frowned on by the pleasure-hating Puritans, and was finally forbidden by Parliament in 1644, when a decree went out that all the Maypoles were to be uprooted.

For centuries morris dancing was an essential part of village events. Although it is no longer closely linked to village life, there are many groups, or 'teams', still to be found keeping the tradition alive, and adding jollity and colour to the English summer scene.

In York each summer the Mystery Plays are performed by amateur actors of all ages. They are a series of plays dramatizing the Bible from the Creation to the Day of Judgement. Begun in the fourteenth century, this was one of the earliest forms of street theatre, with each company performing a different pageant and the audience following it around the town.

Equally dramatic, and a great outing for small boys, is the Royal Tournament at Earls Court in July. Mounted annually to raise money for the charities of the armed forces, it was first held over one hundred years ago. It is a spectacular show, which includes an exciting race between two teams from the Royal Navy who have to disassemble a field gun, carry it over an obstacle course using only their own hands, and then reassemble it and fire it. The name of the winning team at the end of the fortnight is flashed to all the Navy's ships around the world. The Redcaps, the Royal Military Police, perform tricks with horses and motorcycles and provide plenty of excitement for little boys to dream of in the months to come.

A Country Weekend

ACCORDING to Jack Worthing in Oscar Wilde's *The Importance of Being Earnest*, when one is in town one amuses oneself, when one is in the country one amuses other people. Weekending in the country is very enjoyable, even if the days have surely gone when the guests would be met at the local station by the chauffeur in a Rolls-Royce, and have their bags unpacked by a manservant such as Jeeves. One of the funniest books I have ever read is A. G. Macdonell's *England, Their England* . It tells the story of a naïve young writer trying to write a book about the English, and contains the following description by a bright young thing of a 'typical' country weekend party:

Arriving at the Norman manor of Faulconhurst St Honoré at midday on Saturday, he drinks absinthe cocktails and exchanges dazzling epigrams until luncheon with others of his own age and brilliance, all about the Hollowness of Life, the Folly of the Old, the Comicality of the War, the Ideas of the Young, the Brilliance of the Young, the Superiority of Modern Photography over Velazquez, and the Futility of People of Forty. After luncheon, which consists of quails and foie gras and sparkling Burgundy, with sherbet for the teetotallers, and pomegranates and persimmons and a glass of Avocat, there are more epigrams until cocktails again at 4.30, and finally the exhausted epigrammatists retire to their virtuous couches at about 3 a.m. to rise again at noon on Sunday for a breakfast of aspirin and absinthe, and another day of brilliance.

This may be a slight exaggeration, but as a guest one is expected to sing for one's supper by at least talking to one's table companions on either side, even if one has little in common with them. Between meals the country gentleman fills the day by participating in some form of sport. He may watch his daughter out in the paddock with her ponies practising for a forthcoming gymkhana, or play a game of lawn tennis with his guests. Croquet on the lawn is a favourite pursuit for those who do not take their

sport seriously — as well as some who do — whereas a game of cricket on the village green is only for those who do take their sport seriously.

If there is a Test match in progress, the English Gentleman is sure to be in one of only two places. Either at Lord's, watching the match from the Pavilion, or in front of the television with the sound turned down listening to the commentary on Radio 5. There are many unmistakable sounds of summer — bees buzzing round the hives, birds twittering in the hedgerows; what captures an English summer for me, however, is the sound of leather on willow, accompanied by the voice of Brian Johnston.

In the country house one was expected to dress for dinner, which meant smoking jacket and black tie for gentlemen and an evening dress for ladies. Nowadays this only happens on special occasions. At the end of the stay there are two duties to be done. A tip has to be left for the staff, and on arriving home a bread and butter letter has to be written to say thank you.

A Most Civilized Meal

... Oh! yet
Stands the Church clock at ten to three?
And is there honey still for tea?

RUPERT BROOKE

TEA is a most civilized meal; it can expand to include a light supper dish such as coddled eggs or cheese on toast, or be a simple cup of Earl Grey with a slice of lemon. For me the presentation is all important. This is the moment for the starched damask cloth and the embroidered napkins, and I am very fond of lace doilies underneath my cakes. I select my tea rather as I select my perfume — to match my mood and the season. In winter I may have Lapsang Souchong or Gunpowder Green, whereas in summer I prefer something a little lighter, such as Jasmine Blossom or Formosa Oolong, which has a hint of peach.

I also enjoy going out for tea, and we are fortunate to have so many good tea shops which cater for this curious English habit. I could have tea every day at Betty's in York or Harrogate and still return for more. After a sandwich or two there is nothing quite like a freshly baked scone with a little butter, lashings of thick Devon cream and strawberry jam or honey. I will always associate honey with Rupert Brooke's poem, 'The Old Vicarage, Grantchester', written in 1912, just three years before his death on the Western Front. Grantchester is a charming village on the River Cam, near Cambridge, and the ideal place for tea during an afternoon's punting on the river.

There are very good tea-shops to be found at the seaside, too, especially in the small fishing villages of Devon and Cornwall. It is fun to watch the fishing boats coming in with the catch, buy fresh cockles and mussels from the stall at the harbour, or eat fish and chips out of newspaper on the sea front. This is the area about which Daphne du Maurier wrote so hauntingly in her novels *Frenchman's Creek* and *Rebecca*.

The Seaside

I went down to the shouting sea,
Taking Christopher down with me,
For Nurse had given us sixpence each —
And down we went to the beach

A. A. MILNE

MILNE's poem about Christopher Robin paints a wonderfully evocative picture of the English seaside. One of my clearest memories of the seaside is of sitting on the beach with the wind blowing. We would pore over the wireless the evening before we were due to go to the sea, listening to the BBC weather forecast for shipping. Dover, Rockall, Shannon, Portland, Biscay, Plymouth, Finistere — the names of distant lighthouses became second nature to us, but might have been in a foreign language for all the sense they made.

When the sun is shining there is nowhere nicer than an English seaside town. There are pretty pastel beach huts to be hired, and sand castles to be built, rock pools in which to paddle, donkeys to ride and ice creams to be had from the ice-cream man on the sea-front ringing his bell. A Punch and Judy show is always popular with children, and the small shops sell buckets and spades, shrimping nets and bright pink rock. In the bigger resorts there is a pier and a summer show at the theatre. There are arcades and slot machines and trick photographic booths where you can have your photograph taken as a can-can dancer, sailor or whatever. Around the coast there are many such resorts, but for us children the best treat of the summer holidays was to go to Blackpool to see the coloured lights above the streets, known as the 'illuminations'. On arrival there was never any doubt about what we wanted to do first — visit the fun-fair and go on the Big Dipper. There were many rides and we were happy to stay all day, throwing balls at coconuts, having a go on the dodgems and riding the merry-go-round. Later, when it grew dark, the illuminations came on and we drove the car through the town to see them. It was long past our bedtime, which already made it a very special occasion, but to see the coloured balls light up and make scenes above our heads was truly magical.

Roses and Silver

And when you plant your rose trees, plant them deep,
Having regard to bushes all aflame,
And see the dusky promise of their bloom
In small red shoots, and let each redolent name –
Tuscany, Crested Cabbage, Cottage Maid –
Load with full June November's dank repose;
See the kind cattle drowsing in the shade
And hear the bee about his amorous trade,
Brown in the gypsy crimson on the rose.

VITA SACKVILLE-WEST

WHEN I see bunches of identical red roses sold on the street corner, I feel a certain despair: I know that they have been forced in a distant hothouse, all their perfume will have been bred out of them, and within a couple of days they will hang their heads and die. Commercial rose-growing is here to stay, but happily we have some wonderful nurseries in England, such as Roses du Temps Passé, which specialize in old roses. I have agonized over the selection. Should I allow Bobby James to ramble over our Guest House, or would Rambling Rector be a better size? Will Alfred Carrière look too cool against a dark wall — would I be safer with Zephirine Drouhin? Should I create a separate rose garden, or should I include roses in the herbaceous border? The only way to decide is to visit some gardens and seek advice from old-fashioned nurserymen. What I have learned is that whatever the aspect, soil or situation, whether a shrub rose is required, a climber or a miniature, the perfect rose can always be found. I am fond of the dark red Gallica roses with their velvety petals, which bring the most wonderful scent into the house. I fill the silver rose bowl with a variety of different coloured roses, and spread goblets and tankards around the house, on side tables, mantelpieces and wash-stands, so bringing the glory of the summer garden into the home.

I have always loved small silver objects, perhaps as a result of having a silver charm bracelet and collecting charms as a small girl. It has to shine, which means lots of polishing, but having a small collection seems to me to be a nice easy way to bring a little luxury into our lives. We use silver rings for our table napkins and the children drink their milk out of their silver Christening mugs. Photographs of family and friends are in silver frames on top of the piano, and around the house and we have silver brushes on our dressing tables and washstands. We always dine by candlelight, and the table often has small posies of fresh flowers from the garden in silver posy holders. None of these is particularly valuable, but they give me a great deal of pleasure for they are not only beautifully made but full of memories. As I pour my tea in the morning I think of the aunts who gave us the tea service when we were married, or of my grandparents, whose initials are still on our silver napkin rings. I love to look for unusual presents for friends, and try to find small pieces of silver which are amusing and right for the occasion. I searched and searched to find something for my old schoolfriend who had a special birthday coming up, and just as I thought I was never going to find anything, there on the stall in the market in front of my eyes was a small silver box with the inscription: 'I'll love my friend, unto the end'. As I was paying for it a tiny silver box in the shape of a book caught my eye — the perfect gift for my publisher.

Picnics

PICNICS are an essential part of the English summer, whether it is a romantic picnic for two, sitting on a travelling rug in a remote beauty spot, or champagne and caviar served by the butler out of the boot of the Rolls-Royce. There are plenty of occasions for the latter during the Season, the first being the Fourth of June celebrations at Eton College. This is really an open day for parents, but once prayers have been said and the speeches are over, everyone is free to socialize. The picnic is likely to be served on china plates out of a wicker basket, and the spread will include traditional English summer fare: smoked salmon, lobster, asparagus and chicken, followed by strawberries and cream with Pimms or champagne to drink.

The picnic basket remains out for the rest of the summer. Royal Ascot in June, and the Henley Regatta, in July, both provide an opportunity for English society to dress up.

Other highlights of the Season include Cowes Regatta in August, the great sailing event of the year, which takes place off the Isle of Wight, and racing at Goodwood. My own personal favourite of all these occasions is Glyndebourne, where music-lovers go to see opera performed in a small opera house in the middle of the Sussex Downs.

My favourite description of a picnic is in *The Wind in the Willows*, when the Water Rat introduces Mole to the delights of a picnic on the river:

'Hold hard a minute, then!' said the Rat. He looped the painter through a ring in his landing-stage, climbed up into his hole above, and … reappeared staggering under a fat, wicker luncheon-basket.

'Shove that under your feet,' he observed to the Mole, as he passed it down into the boat. Then he untied the painter and took the sculls again.

What's inside it?' asked the Mole, wriggling with curiosity.

'There's cold chicken inside it,' replied the Rat briefly; 'coldtonguecoldham-coldbeefpickledgherkinssaladfrenchrollscresssandwidgepottedmeatgingerbeerlemon-adesodawater —'

The Country Cottage

'Mid pleasures and palaces though we may roam,
Be it ever so humble, there's no place like home!
A charm from the skies seems to hallow us there,
Which seek through the world, ne'er is met with
elsewhere.

Home! home! sweet, sweet home!
There's no place like home, there's no place like home!

An exile from home, splendour dazzles in vain,
O give me my lowly thatched cottage again!
The birds singing gaily, that came at my call,
Give me them, with the peace of mind dearer than all.

ANON

THATCHING is an old craft practised in the country where houses have had thatched roofs for centuries. The houses are timber framed, and sheaves of Norfolk reed are tied by rope to the rafters. Layers and layers of reed or long wheat straw are fixed on top with willow twigs bent into a hoop. On the very top is the layer for the ridge, and the end is cut into a special shape which is the thatcher's signature. Some thatchers put a straw animal on the roof to help identify the building, and there is a Swan Inn I know which has a swan sitting on the top. This love of animals extends also to topiary and in the country one often sees box hedges and trees in the shape of chickens and rabbits as well as more eccentric creations. The art of topiary is said to have been invented at the time of Augustus Caesar and has been popular in England for centuries. This may be because privet, yew and box flourish in our climate,

but also because according to folklore topiary figures kept evil spirits at bay. It is not a pastime for the impatient, however, for it can take years for the hedging to grow but just weeks to grow out of shape — as I found to my cost when I took my eye off a twisted conical box tree and found that it had grown into a cone.

Whenever I drive through the villages of Suffolk or the Cotswolds, I am charmed by the cottage gardens I see. Part of their appeal is that no formal design has gone into their planting, and colourful old-fashioned flowers grow happily alongside vegetables and herbs underneath fruit trees. Traditional names abound: Snapdragons, Monkshood, Granny Bonnets, Lamb's Ears and Blue-Eyed Mary. The cottage garden as we know it evolved over the centuries. Until the reign of Henry VIII medicinal herbs were grown by monks in the cloisters; with the dissolution of the monasteries villagers had to grow herbs and spices in their own gardens. So angelica was introduced and used to help poor circulation, caraway to aid digestion and comfrey to cure bronchitis.

In the late eighteenth century the Enclosure Acts forced landowners to reduce the size of many gardens; consequently cottagers who were dependent upon their garden for food crammed rows of vegetables between the herbs and flowers. There was usually a bee-hive which produced delicious sweet-smelling honey, and roses and honeysuckle ramble up the walls, almost covering the leaded windows. The path is barely visible between the closely-packed plants and the gate is constantly open for the garden is so friendly.

English Lavender

'Twas on a Monday morning
When I beheld my darling,
She looked so neat and charming
In ev'ry high degree;
She looked so neat and nimble, O,
A-washing of her linen, O,
Dashing away with the smoothing iron,
Dashing away with the smoothing iron,
Dashing away with the smoothing iron,
She stole my heart away.

SOMERSET FOLK SONG

I have dedicated this book to my American friend Janet, because of her deep love and appreciation for all things English. Whenever I go and stay with her I find a tablet of Old English Lavender soap on my washstand. The first thing I do when I see it is to pick it up, turn it over and breathe in the wonderful aroma. I am immediately transported back to the vast mahogany linen cupboard where my mother kept her linen in neat rows, scented by lavender bags. Each week on wash day, piles of linen sheets, newly starched pillow cases and hand towels would be arranged on the shelves, just as they had been by her mother and grandmother before her. Many things were from her trousseau and had been made or decorated by her family. The pillow cases all had deep lacy borders from an aunt who specialized in tatting; the hand towels had beautiful faggoting along their borders, or were embroidered with ladies wearing crinoline dresses surrounded by hollyhocks. Many had initials from past generations, from an age when white bedlinen was *de rigueur* and things were made to last. But all carried the same delicate scent of lavender.

Scenting our clothes and linen is by no means a recent custom. In Elizabethan times the lady of the house grew the herbs she needed in beautiful knot gardens, then gathered them, dried them and used them in cooking or made them into medicines. Lavender was one of the principal herbs in her garden and was sometimes strewn on the floor to scent the air. Garlands of lavender were made and hung over the fireplace; it was one of the main ingredients of her pot-pourri, and helped to keep the moths out of her clothes.

Today there are many varieties of lavender from which to choose, and the plants which produce the finest scent in the world are grown in Norfolk. When we moved into our London home we were delighted to find an ancient variety, Twickle Purple, which grew up through a cotoneaster so high that I had to use a step-ladder to gather it. No matter how plentiful the harvest, however, I never seemed to have enough to make lavender bags for my own linen press, to put amongst our clothes and to tie in bunches to give to friends. At the top of the lawn we had planted a blue herbaceous border without realizing that it would be behind the stumps when my son, James, played cricket. When we saw the delphiniums going down like soldiers, we knew we had to move the plants and replace them with something sturdy enough to withstand the onslaught of a ten-year-old's bowling. We planted *Lavandula stoechas*, which is small and stocky, and surrounded it with box hedging. I now have enough lavender to satisfy my needs, and James can bowl to his heart's content.

As soon as the weather is really warm we like to eat outside. This sometimes begins on a sunny morning when we decide to take our breakfast out and enjoy the fresh air. Quite apart from what my husband David grows for me in his vegetable garden, there is a wealth of fresh produce in the market — the essence of summer fare is freshness and seasonality.

Often the most simple dish is the most effective. A selection of different salads, radicchio, red lettuce and frisee, tossed with coriander and an olive oil dressing served on plain white china is the perfect start to dinner. It is also easily prepared, and Charlotte Rose, our nine-year-old daughter does it very well.

Cold soups can also be delicious and simple to make. Cucumber, watercress, courgette, sorrel, all make wonderful soups and look beautiful in white bowls. With a swirl of fresh cream or yoghurt in the centre and decorated with a sprig of watercress, cold soup is the perfect start to a summer lunch dish accompanied by some fresh wholemeal bread. We like to follow with fish or meat grilled over charcoal. I hesitate to use the word barbecue, in case it conjures up visions of blackened sausages or raw chicken drumsticks eaten long past lunch-time. The secret of the barbecue is to have it a long way away from the dining table, so that you cannot smell it, and to start it in plenty of time. The food should not be put on until the grill is really hot, and then watched carefully so that it does not burn. We have grilled red mullet, salmon and even sea bass with success, and we always agree that food does taste better outside.

All through the summer, as different fruits come into season, mouth-watering sweets and puddings can be made. Gooseberry fool, blackberry and apple pie, apricot tart, and a variety of sorbets and ice-cream. However, the dessert which epitomizes summer dining for me is summer pudding — which may be eaten by itself or served with a little fresh, preferably thick cream. The recipe here is for raspberries and redcurrants, but blackberries, strawberries, or any soft summer fruit can also be used.

SUMMER PUDDING

1 lb/450g raspberries
¼ lb/120g redcurrants
¼ lb/120g sugar
White bread, sliced as for sandwiches

Remove the stalks from the redcurrants and remove any bruised fruit. Cook the fruit and sugar together for three minutes, with no water, and leave to cool. Remove the crust from slices of one-day-old white bread and line a pudding basin with it, making sure that there are no gaps. Carefully spoon in the fruit, reserving some of the juice. Cover the fruit completely with bread and place a weighted plate on top. Leave for 24 hours in the refrigerator, then turn out on to a curved dish and pour the remaining liquid over it.

Home‧Grown Produce

WHENEVER I travel by train I enjoy looking out of the carriage window at the allotments which often run down to the railway embankment. Allotments are small pieces of land rented by those with no garden of their own in which to grow flowers and vegetables. I suspect that having a quiet place of one's own in which to potter gives as much satisfaction as growing marvellous vegetables.

Those who take a pride in their garden often enter their produce in horticultural shows, where prizes are awarded for the quality of the exhibits. Outstanding specimens of fruit and vegetables, flower arrangements and preserves are all judged by local experts, and as the produce is usually sold afterwards it is a good way to sample the local fare. The display is often worthy of a Dutch oil painting. Giant striped marrows and orange pumpkins sit amongst bunches of carrots and radishes – the whole display a testimony to healthy eating.

Bazaars and bring-and-buy sales are an excellent source for country produce, the proceeds usually going towards the church steeple fund or the Women's Institute. Home-baked cakes and biscuits, seedlings, cuttings and small bunches of cottage garden flowers sit side by side with chutneys and marmalade. My particular weakness is lemon curd, or lemon cheese as it is sometimes called, and I can never resist buying it. It is delicious spread on fresh bread as a teatime treat.

LEMON CURD

Makes 2 x 1 lb jam-jars
4 oz/120g/8 tbsp butter
8 oz/240g/1 cup granulated sugar
3 eggs, plus 1 extra yolk
3 medium-sized lemons

Melt butter in the top of a double saucepan. Add sugar, beaten eggs and finely grated rind and juice of lemons. Cook gently without boiling until curd thickens sufficiently to coat the back of the spoon. (Do not overheat or it will curdle and separate.) Pour into clean, dry, warm jam-jars and cover as for jam. Store in a very cool place and eat within two weeks.

This Little Space

something which takes my breath away. Whether it is the Nuttery in the spring, planted with red and yellow polyanthus, the white garden in midsummer, or The Moat Walk in winter with the statue of Dionysius reflected in the water, one cannot but admire their vision and the sheer size of their undertaking. I never manage to take in the whole garden in one visit, the beauty of it is so overpowering. It is visited by thousands of visitors each year. I often wonder if others go home and move their plants around the garden as I do.

The great gardening event of the year which attracts thousands of visitors is the Chelsea Flower Show. Set in the grounds of the Royal Hospital at Chelsea, it is the annual show of The Royal Horticultural Society, and all the famous nurseries

This little space which scented box encloses
Is blue with lupins and is sweet with thyme,
My garden all is overblown with roses,
My spirit all is overblown with roses,
My spirit all is overblown with rhyme,
As like a drunken honeybee I waver
From house to garden and again to house,
And, undetermined which delight to favour,
On verse and rose alternately carouse.

VITA SACKVILLE-WEST

ANYBODY who has ever visited Sissinghurst Castle in Kent will probably, like me, have fallen under its spell. It was the creation of Vita Sackville-West and her husband, the diplomat and writer, Harold Nicolson. I have visited Sissinghurst at all seasons and there is always

exhibit there, displaying their specialities. I am always amazed that daffodils, delphiniums and chrysanthemums are all in bloom at the same time, but all the growers manage to force or hold back their blooms so that they are at their peak for mid-May when the Chelsea Flower Show takes place. There is usually a good display of landscaping by one of the London parks. I rather regret the way in which, like many of the arts, gardening has become so much more sophisticated over the past decade. I used to love the round beds in the local park which I passed on the way to the swings, with white alyssum, blue lobelia and red salvia — bedded out each year — in the shape of a clock.

The gardens at Buckingham Palace are a curious mixture of formal rose-gardens, herbaceous borders, a lake with flamingoes and acres of wild garden. There are parts which are quite public and other areas such as the Pet's Graveyard, where the Queen's dogs are buried, which feel very private. For anyone privileged to be invited to one of Her Majesty's Garden Parties, a stroll through the grounds of the Palace listening to the Band playing is a delightful way of passing the afternoon. She invites people from all walks of life. Tea is served, the National Anthem is played, and the Queen comes out into the garden with members of the Royal Family to walk among her guests.

AUTUMN

Harvest awakes the morning still,
And toil's rude groups the valleys fill;
Deserted is each cottage hearth
To all life, save the cricket's mirth;
Each burring wheel its sabbeth meets,
Nor walks a gossip in the streets;
The bench beneath the eldern bough,
Lined o'er with grass, is empty now,
Where blackbirds, caged from out of the sun,
Would whistle while their mistress spun:
All haunt the thronged fields, to share
The harvest's lingering bounty there. ...

JOHN CLARE

On returning home after the summer holiday there is always a slight chill in the morning air, telling us that autumn is on its way. On the grouse moors the guns and beaters have been stalking through the heather since 'the glorious twelfth' of August and in City restaurants the small birds, so eagerly awaited, are now being enjoyed. Covered in bacon and roasted, served with forcemeat balls, breadcrumbs and game chips, the grouse is without equal. It is said to be an acquired taste, for it is the most gamy of all the birds, but it is a great favourite in our family.

The sign that autumn is really here is the migration of the birds. At the beginning of September the swifts usually begin to leave, and for the next month the swallows collect on the telegraph wires. Their departure is dramatic. After weeks of twittering and swooping they gather together in a large mass which hangs in the sky like a dark cloud before finally moving off to warmer climes.

September also sees the start of the Michaelmas term, the first of three in the academic year. New boys and girls nervously approach the stately buildings of our great schools, some founded as long ago as the sixteenth century. Each school has its own traditions and character, but all strive to give the pupils a broad education in mind, body and spirit. For centuries the school chapels have rung out with the hymns of John Bunyan and Charles Wesley, and to this day I cannot sing my own school hymn without a lump in my throat, remembering the pride and respect for which it stood.

> Our Father, by whose servants
> Our house was built of old,
> Whose hand hath crowned her children
> With blessings manifold,
> For Thine unfailing mercies
> Far-strewn along our way,
> With all who passed before us,
> We praise Thy name to-day.

At the end of September the academic elite will be taking their places at Oxford and Cambridge, our great seats of learning, for three years of study interspersed with the irresponsible fun of student life.

By September the Promenade Concerts at the Royal Albert Hall in London are well under way. Begun in 1895 by Sir Henry Wood, the Proms are an immensely popular and egalitarian institution. Those who cannot afford seats are able to sit on the floor at the front or around the top level of the domed concert hall. The world-famous Last Night of the Proms contains old favourites such as Blake's 'Jerusalem', 'Rule Britannia', and 'Land of Hope and Glory', and the audience is encouraged to participate.

R o y a l   O a k   T r e e s

IT is said that the heel of the year is always golden and autumn is famous for her colours. In our garden the small delicate acers turn deep crimson, and the colour is echoed on the other side of the garden where hydrangea heads are turning red and papery. Every year I watch out for this moment, so that I can cut and dry them and use them to add colour indoors when fresh flowers are not so plentiful.

This is the time of the year when I cut back the herbaceous plants which have finished flowering so that on warm days we can still enjoy late-blooming plants. The creeping campanula which grows wild in the garden has come out for a second showing, and the sedum has at last come into her own. I like to have several clumps of sedum in the garden so that I can cut some and bring them indoors, where they look very ornamental on the hall table in a big Chinese vase.

Autumn is the season for harvesting, starting with the lavender. There are berries to be gathered, fruit to be picked and the last of the vegetables to be removed from the vegetable garden before it is dug over. Autumn has a very particular smell of newly dug earth, rotting leaves and bonfires. Before the first frost the geraniums and begonias have to be brought indoors, and I plant wallflowers in their place. I try to plant a single colour, which is how I prefer them, but one or two of a different colour always seem to find their way in there and they do not like being moved. Once the clocks go back and it is dark by tea-time, I think of the bulbs which need to be planted if we are to have bowls of white hyacinth and narcissus for early January.

All through the season the leaves never stop falling, and no matter how often we sweep them up the lawn is always covered. Oak trees are sometimes deemed to be the symbol of England, and have been known as Royal Oaks since 1651, when, following defeat in battle, King Charles II hid in an oak tree to avoid being found by Cromwell's troops. I have always liked to see oak trees in the autumn when their green leaves have changed to rust. Their silhouette is instantly recognizable, and with their gnarled branches and leaves like russet petticoats they are the most romantic of trees.

A T r a n q u i l S p o r t

ALTHOUGH hunting, shooting and fishing are considered to be the sports of an English country gentleman, they are enjoyed by all kinds of people. Even in towns, canal banks are full of small boys eager to learn the art of fishing. They begin by catching sticklebacks and tiddlers with a net and jam-jar, but very soon have graduated to a rod and reel and are angling for roach and carp. David, my husband, made his own rod for coarse fishing out of Spanish reed when he was fifteen and proudly brought it to our new home when we married.

Those of us who are not caught up in the spell of this quiet tranquil sport wonder where the magic lies, as hours slip by and no fish rise to the bait.

While to the onlooker little seems to happen, fishermen are rarely bored. Life on the river is never still and there are many things to catch the eye. A brilliant blue kingfisher may suddenly fly by, or you might see otters playing. Dealing with the tackle would be enough to keep most of us occupied. I particularly like the artificial flies with their romantic names – Waddington Elverine, Esmond Drury Logie, Stoat's Tail and Orange. I remember accompanying David on a fishing trip to Scotland and stopping for a cup of tea at a hotel on Loch Maree. In the entrance hall the fishermen and gillies were crowded round a small showcase discussing the contents. The title of the exhibition was 'Flies by Kenneth'.

Fly tying is an art in itself, and fly fishing is undoubtedly the most sophisticated form of the sport, whether it be for trout on the River Test in Hampshire or for salmon in Scotland. It entails great skill, thought and patience. Strength is an asset but not essential, as Queen Elizabeth, the Queen Mother, proved. She fished for salmon, wading out into the river, until well into her eighties. Much of the excitement is in the anticipation, for the sensation of playing a big fish is an experience not easily forgotten.

Baking Day

THERE was a time when English women would set aside a day each week for baking. They would begin by leaving the yeast to rise for the bread and rolls, and then go on to make the scones, pies and cakes which have always made tea in England so delicious. The pantry had cupboards full of cake tins and baking trays, for there is a correct size and shape for every item. Mrs Beeton, a nineteenth-century English cookery writer whose book *Household Management* has become a classic guide to Victorian cookery, lists one dozen tartlette-tins and three dozen round patty-pans, fluted, as essential kitchen utensils in 1912, together with raised pie moulds, paste jaggers and a box of assorted fancy cutters.

While we are all familiar nowadays with Bakewell tarts, small round Eccles cakes and swirling Chelsea buns, their names indicate their origin, and baking remains to some extent a regional art. I so enjoy a tea-cake or a butty when I am in Yorkshire, and yet one hundred miles south you are unlikely to find either of them. As a child we never had to make oatcakes for the oatcake man came round once a week selling them from a large bag. They were large, flat and crumbly, and to this day I have only to smell oatcakes cooking and I think of him. A weekly treat was apple pie, always served with a slab of cheddar cheese; another was bilberry pie, which turned our mouths purple.

Cakes, too, tended to be seasonal. In the winter we had buttered maltloaf for tea, or gingerbread, with any leftover mixture being made into gingerbread men. In summer a lighter cherry cake would be baked, or a Victoria sponge cake with cream and strawberries in the centre. Queen cakes, maids of honour, shortbread, macaroons and meringues were all made at home, but sometimes, for our parties, we were allowed to go to Mr Clay's bakery and make a selection. There large wooden trays contained miniature bridge rolls, iced buns with cherries on the top, small treacle tarts, coconut pyramids and eclairs — it was a child's paradise. Nursery tea in England is an institution.

A Well-Stocked Pantry

WHEN the garden begins to slow down in the autumn we are able to take some time away from tending the flower garden and reap the benefit of our labours in the fruit garden earlier in the year. This is a busy time in the kitchen, for as the different fruits mature, they need to be picked and preserved. I am completely dependent upon a small, nondescript-looking book, *The Country Housewife's Handbook*, published in the 1930s by the Federation of Women's Institutes.

Every fruit has its own characteristics and requirements, and my little book lists them all. The quince, for example, like the medlar, should not be picked until the middle of November, following several frosts. If it had not been for the book, I would have been out there with my basket pulling them off the trees before the frost came. Nor would I have known that cobnuts should be laid in an airy place for a week or two and turned at intervals to prevent mildew. Pears turn a paler shade of green when they are ready to be picked, and like apples should be picked off the tree before they fall.

Fruit may be preserved by being bottled whole, made into jams, jellies, syrups, pickles and chutneys, or being crystallized or dried. The golden rule for preserving fruit is 'One hour from the garden to the pot'. The fruit must be ripe and firm, and for best results the fruit should be of uniform size. Thereafter, close attention to the method is all-important. Watching the pan boil, making the syrup, sealing and sterilizing take time and concentration, but how satisfying it is to put the bottles away on the larder shelf afterwards. Many people now have home freezers, but there is something about the quality of bottled fruit which makes it special and quite different from frozen fruit.

In our family, Monday lunch was often the remains of the joint with baked potatoes, chutneys, pickled onions and piccalilly. This was my grandmother's recipe, which went with my mother when she married. My mother was delighted to find that David enjoyed piccalilly as much as his father-in-law used to do, and she would send a couple of jars down south whenever she made it.

PICCALILLY

Makes 8 x 1 lb jam-jars

1 lb small pickling onions
1 small cauliflower
1 cucumber
1 1 lb marrow
1/2 lb runner beans
4 oz salt
2 1/2 pints water

Peel the onions, leaving them whole. Break the cauliflower into sprigs. Peel the marrow, then remove the inside and cut into small pieces. Peel and slice the cucumber, and cut the beans into inch slices. Cover with brine solution (4 oz salt in 2 1/2 pints water), and leave for 24 hours.

For the Sauce

3 oz plain flour
4 oz caster sugar
2 oz dry mustard
1/2 oz turmeric powder
1 quart vinegar

Put ingredients into pan over a low heat and blend into a paste with a little vinegar. Add remainder of vinegar and stir over heat until boiling and thickened. Add drained vegetables and boil for 5 minutes, stirring all the time. Put into warm jam-jars and cover with paper jam covers. Keep in a cool place

A L i t e r a r y   H e r i t a g e

I was fortunate to grow up in a house where everyone read for pleasure and there were always lots of books. The Yorkshire moors are bleak and lonely, and the holidays would have seemed long without visits to Boots lending library. When my aunts said that they were only giving me a book token for my birthday or Christmas I was overjoyed, for this meant a trip to the bookshop and perhaps the discovery of a new author.

As a student I had little money for books, but I discovered the world of antiquarian bookshops, which were to become a lifelong passion. Small dark rooms, lined from floor to ceiling with books, were presided over by learned men who were willing to find a certain edition of book for me in order to complete a series, if they did not have it in stock. They specialized in first editions, but outside the shop there was always a shelf or two of books with little value through which to browse. I soon found that for the price of a new hardback book I could buy a second-hand one, perhaps with the original illustrations, and sometimes leather-bound. Paperbacks are a wonderful modern convenience for the beach or the 'plane, but for me reading takes on an extra dimension when the words are printed in an old typeface and on beautiful paper. When travelling I could never resist going into antiquarian bookshops, and slowly I built up a collection of our great English authors and playwrights.

William Shakespeare, England's greatest dramatist and poet, was born in 1564 in Stratford-upon-Avon, a small country town on the River Avon in Warwickshire. His writing has maintained its popularity for nearly four hundred years. A great story-teller, he often chose historical subjects, and seeing the plays today one is invariably struck by the relevance of his arguments. His themes are timeless, and many of our everyday sayings originated in his work.

I have always been interested in the Brontës, for they lived in Haworth, which is 'just over the tops' from Hebden Bridge. Charlotte, Emily, Anne and their brother Branwell lived in the stone parsonage with a view over the moors. They were all writers, and I have often wondered who was the inspiration for the wild character of Heathcliff in Emily's *Wuthering Heights*, a dramatic, romantic novel set in a bleak farmhouse on the moors.

A century later, Trollope and Dickens had both begun their vast output of novels. Dickens created great characters and stories which embraced the whole spectrum of society, but was fascinated by the lives of the working classes in Victorian London. Anthony Trollope worked for the Post Office for most of his life, getting up at dawn to write his great chronicles, which have become some of our best-loved books.

Dark Satanic Mills

And did those feet in ancient time
Walk upon England's mountains green?
And was the holy Lamb of God
On England's pleasant pastures seen?

And did the Countenance Divine
Shine forth upon our clouded hills?
And was Jerusalem builded here
Among those dark Satanic Mills?

WILLIAM BLAKE

THE towns and villages of the West Riding of Yorkshire, built along the valleys beneath the bleak Yorkshire moors, are dark and dramatic. They were not always dark: the grimness of the sooty buildings beside the canals came from decades of dirty smoke pouring out of the tall chimneys of the textile mills which have been a feature of the industrial landscape since the beginning of the nineteenth century.

The textile industry has dictated the social structure of the county since the days when sheep were kept by the abbeys and manors, and the wool was sold to foreign merchants at wool fairs and then exported from York and Hull. Such was the demand from the Continent that raw material began to be made into cloth at home. The woollen industry still dominates the West Riding, and the Wool Exchange in Bradford is the centre where the mill owners go to buy the raw wool.

In the manufacture of wool there are many processes between the sheep's back and a gentleman's suit, and up and down the valleys, where many small firms do the specialist jobs, there is much talk of top making, wool combing, spinning, twisting, winding and warping.

My mother's family had a mill of a slightly more specialized nature. Maude's Clog Soles supplied the soles for the clogs worn by the northern mill workers. It was always a treat to visit Uncle Harold in his oak-panelled office — samples of wooden clog soles on his desk, his pockets full of jelly babies. As a small child he remembered his father standing in the window of Carr House, tears pouring down his cheeks as he watched the clog mill burn down. One of my mother's proudest possessions is the gold clock the Bank gave to my grandfather when he had repaid all the money which they lent him to rebuild it.

Family Albums

SMALL boys' pockets are always full of pebbles, sticks and rubber bands, and little girls love to collect postcards, china ornaments and theatre programmes. We get into the habit of collecting from an early age and while our tastes change, the joy and satisfaction remains with us. Stamps, photographs, butterflies, cigarette cards, toby jugs and autographs are just a few of the items which are eagerly collected by people of all ages.

The English have always been collectors, often as a result of having travelled. In the eighteenth and early nineteenth century, at the time of the Grand Tour, they returned with paintings and statues from Renaissance Italy and classical Greece and began the important collections for which many of our stately homes are celebrated today. These collections are part of our national heritage, and the combination of silks and rich textiles from India and the East, Persian carpets, porcelain, marble busts and fine European furniture have become known as *le style anglais* and is widely copied today, from Madison Avenue to the Faubourg St Honoré.

How to preserve these great collections in the future, now that many of the families that owned them no longer have the resources to do so themselves, is a major problem. The National Trust is a fine organization which has preserved many fine properties for the nation, but in order to take one on it insists on a substantial endowment, and the impoverished aristocracy does not always have the funds available even for that. The result is that parts of collections have to be sold off or, tragically, whole collections such as the one at Mentmore are broken up. I feel it is our duty as a nation to find a way to preserve such a wonderful heritage, for it is irreplaceable.

Harvest Festival

ODAY the baskets of apples and fresh vegetables sit beside tins of processed peas and sliced peaches on the church windowsill at Harvest Festival, but the sentiment is still as strong. It is a season of relief and thanksgiving for the safe gathering of the crops. In the preceding weeks, the farmers have been anxiously tapping the barometer, hoping that the good weather will hold so that they can harvest their crops before the autumn rain arrives.

Not only was the harvest crucial to the farmer's livelihood, then as now; it was also an event of great conviviality. The farmer's wife would provide large flagons of home-brewed cider and giant wheels of cheddar cheese as refreshment during the day, and at night there would be a simple rustic feast when all the work was done.

Farmers today no longer scythe by hand, they use large combine harvesters, but the traditions remain the same, and Harvest Festival continues to be an important event in the church calendar. Everyone in the congregation makes a contribution and brings it to the service. The age-old hymns, 'We plough the fields and scatter' and 'Come, ye thankful people come' are sung; on the altar are symbols of life, a large plait of bread and some water, and the church looks festive, decorated with wheatsheaves and local produce.

Throughout the world, harvest has always been the occasion for odd customs, and in England to this day vestiges of magic may still be found. At the close of reaping in Northumberland, when the last sheaf is set on end, the reapers shout that they have 'got the kern'. It is then dressed in a white frock and hoisted on to a pole. The Kern baby is then carried back in triumph and set up in a prominent place during the harvest supper. In Devon an old man selects a bundle of good ears of wheat, which is called 'the neck', then the reapers stand around him in a ring. They take off their hats and hold them with both hands towards the ground. Then all together they cry 'The Neck!' three times, standing up with their hats high above their heads. This is called 'crying the neck' and is one of many symbolic ceremonies which have remained long after their origins have been forgotten.

WINTER

Yet but awhile the slumbering weather flings
Its murky prison round — then winds wake loud;
With sudden stir the startled forest sings
Winter's returning song — cloud races cloud,
And the horizon throws away its shroud,
Sweeping a stretching circle from the eye;
Storms upon storms in quick succession crowd,
And o'er the sameness of the purple sky
Heaven paints, with hurried hand, wild hues of every dye.

JOHN CLARE

WHEN the ground is covered with a white hoary frost we know that winter has arrived, and one almost envies the small animals who just curl up and hibernate. Now that the leafless trees are exposed in their naked beauty, the landscape takes on a new aspect. The wintry sun shines feebly through the branches and retires early, disappearing over the horizon like an orange or crimson ball. The ground is hard and crisp, and if there is ice on the pond, the bluetits will peck through the tinsel tops of the milk bottles for their morning drink. The harsh frost forms a pattern of opalescent crushed velvet on our window panes which slowly dissolves in the morning sun.

The winter garden has a strange ethereal beauty but is by no means devoid of colour. Dry crimson hydrangea heads sit beside the elegant long grey tassles of *Garrya elliptica*, and the small sweetly-scented white pompom blossoms of viburnum, when cut and brought indoors, add a Japanese quality to the drawing room. We see once again the old brick walls of the garden against which lean the long arched branches of *cotoneaster lactea* holding clumps of red berries. The gnarled quince tree is still bearing the last of her yellow fruit, and

the corkscrew hazel, with its twisted branches, looks eerily over the pond.

The trees come into their own at this time of the year, their architectural shapes setting the seasonal mood. In our garden we are fortunate to have two ancient plane trees which hang their branches down over our heads like long swaying arms. Their trunks are covered with ivy, the sinister berries shining darkly in the winter sun. The bay, *Laurus nobilis*, stands tall and proud; the silver birch looks ethereal with its white glistening trunk; and the dogwood, stripped of its leaves, shows off a shiny red spotted bark.

We do not tend to think of winter as a season of flowers, with the possible exception of *Helleborus niger*, the Christmas Rose. The large pure white flowers with their golden stamens grow on long stems in clumps under the trees, and I like to surround them with different varieties of euphorbia and lime green *Helleborus corsicus* and *foetidus*. While I set great store by a tidy garden, I love the straggly winter countryside with frosty hedgrows full of scarlet rose hips, silver teasels, and brambles as delicate as a spider's web. The landscape has a lunar quality, quiet and secretive.

Frost and Snow

AND then the snow comes. It masks the familiar outlines with a white cloak which reflects blinding light, and it is only by the tell-tale footprints in the snow that we know that animal life continues. Even with snow on the ground there is work for the gardener to do. Shrubs and small trees need to have the snow shaken from their branches, for the combined weight of those featherlight flakes can be devastating. Logs need to be carried indoors for the fire, and those birds who have braved our English winter need water and nuts to see them through.

This is the moment to make plans for the year ahead. Catalogues from nurseries and seed merchants have been arriving through the post for a few weeks now, and nothing is more seductive to the gardener than the descriptions they contain. Sitting up in bed eagerly reading Margery Fish or Beth Chatto's catalogues of unusual plants, I am immediately transported into the future by the promise of the floral delights the garden has in store. Looking at all the possibilities available is part of the fun and challenge of gardening and now is the time, when the garden seems tranquil and dormant, to be considering them.

Yet even when the snow has lain thick on the ground for weeks, signs start to appear which show that Nature's annual cycle is beginning. Snowdrops push their green spears up to break the crust before letting us see their white bells, and these are followed by czar violets, aconites and the small winter iris. Once the berried Christmas foliage has been taken down on Twelfth Night (6 January), I like to go out into the garden and cut flowers and greenery to put indoors. The red-veined, heart-shaped leaves of epimedium and the russet leaves of the foam-flower, tiarella, are the right size to put in posy jars with the first garden flowers of the season, and the starry branches of yellow winter jasmine bring a pleasing scent and a feeling of new life to the house at the beginning of the new year.

Around the Fire

WHEN the days are short and night draws in at tea-time, English family life centres around the fire. We love to sit here and roast chestnuts or toast muffins, or just read the newspapers and talk. For many months of the year we enjoy outdoor activities, but our climate encourages us to stay indoors in winter. What I choose to call my North of England Protestant Work Ethic, which demands that I do not sit down and enjoy myself until all the jobs are done, is often disobeyed at this time, and for me there is nothing so reassuring on coming home as relaxing with a cat on my knee in front of a log fire.

We are a nation of animal lovers, and the moment the match is put to the kindling, the cat will be there. I have often thought that people are at their nicest when dealing with their pets, and if only we could treat our children and brothers in the same tender way as we handle our dogs and cats, the world would be a much happier place. I have seen tough City gentlemen in their pin-striped suits play like children with a litter of puppies, and it is no secret that the Queen feels most at home with her dogs and horses. She chooses corgis and labradors, but the range of dogs we breed is wide and varied. We can see from ancient portraits that dogs have been kept as pets for centuries.

We all have our favourite animal, and the naming of our pets is a delicate matter. A large grey tomcat who arrived on a friend's doorstep was immediately given dignity by being christened Earl Grey, and Sir Roy Strong writes frequently of the Reverend Wenceslas Muff, who he admits dominates his life. I find that cats usually live up to their names. My first litter of kittens, Peaseblossom, Cobweb, Moth and Mustardseed, behaved as perfect little fairies should. They were swiftly followed by Fortnum, Mason, Marshall, Snelgrove, Debenham and Freebody, the founders of the great department stores of my childhood.

We recently buried our two female tabbies under a small tree at the bottom of the garden. It was a sad occasion, but they were both over twenty years old when they died and their grave is marked by a statue of a small angel. We felt it was unfair to introduce kittens into the home while the old ladies were alive but now the children are eager to go on cat hunts. At the time of writing we have acquired just one, Don Carlos, a smoky grey Maine Coon cat with amber eyes and a large pale grey ruff — hence his name. For me there is nothing to compare with the cat. When I pick him up I know he will purr, he is always waiting for me when I come downstairs in the morning or (reprovingly) when I come in late at night, and his love is unconditional.

Bonfire Night

Remember, remember,
The Fifth of November,
Gunpowder treason and plot.
There is no reason
Why Gunpowder treason
Should ever be forgot!

ANON

ON 5 November 1605, Guy Fawkes and a small band of conspirators planned to blow up King James I and Parliament. However, the plot was revealed, Guy Fawkes was discovered in the cellar of the Houses of Parliament surrounded by casks of gunpowder, and after being tortured he was executed for treason.

Today, nearly four centuries later, we still celebrate the foiling of the Gunpowder Plot with Bonfire Night. Fireworks are let off and for children it is the first treat of winter and one of the most exciting days of the year. For weeks before, small boys go around the villages collecting 'a penny for the guy' and a large bonfire is built of wood. The guy, made of sticks and straw and dressed in old clothes, sits atop the great pyre. At twilight on 5 November, bonfires are lit and fireworks prepared on village greens and in the parks around the land. Roman candles, Catherine wheels and rockets — the names have been the same for generations. Small children watch from the windows and are introduced to the fun and excitement with sparklers, while outside baked potatoes are handed around. A tin of Yorkshire Parkin has always been baked for the occasion, and I am particularly fond of my mother's recipe which manages to be moist yet chewy and guarantees to satisfy hungry children on cold November nights.

YORKSHIRE PARKIN

4 oz/120g/8 tbsp margarine
3 oz/90g/6 tbsp brown sugar
4 heaped tbsp syrup
6 oz/180g/⁷⁄₈ cup self-raising flour
7 oz/210g/1¹⁄₃ cups medium oatmeal
1 egg
¹⁄₂ tsp bicarbonate of soda
1 tsp of ginger
1 small tsp baking powder
Milk

Put all the dry ingredients into a bowl except for the bicarbonate of soda. Put fat, sugar and syrup into a pan and heat over a low flame until just melted. Beat the egg and add it, then add all the dry ingredients. Lastly, dissolve the bicarbonate of soda in a little milk and add to the mixture. The mixture should be of such consistency that you may just pour it into a greased baking tin. If it is too stiff, add a little more milk until you are able to pour the mixture easily. Put the mixture into a 400°F/200°C oven for ten minutes and then reduce heat to 350°F/180°C. Leave in slow oven until firm to the touch. When a skewer comes out cleanly it is cooked. Cut into squares and leave in the tin to cool.

Fine Needlework

IN the novels of Jane Austen ladies often have samplers in their hands, for in her day embroidery was one of the chief pastimes of 'gals' of the leisured classes. Samplers were often worked in a variety of stitches to commemorate a birth or a wedding, and tapestry cushions and chair seats were made to decorate the drawing-rooms of country houses. I was fortunate to work for five years with Franco Zeffirelli in Rome. When I told him that I felt the time had come when I should return to England, he said that I could go when I had stitched four large tapestry cushions for him; I used to take them home with me at night for I was afraid that, like Penelope in Homer's *Odyssey*, he would undo them to postpone the day of completion! Whenever I returned to Rome, I would see them there on his sofa. He often uses things from his home as props for his films, and on seeing his film of *La Traviata* I was moved to tears when Violetta lay on my cushions.

Smocking is a most delicate way of gathering fabric and is often used in making a baby's layette. In my day we wore dresses in Liberty fabric smocked from neck to waist until we were ten or twelve, and there is no prettier sight than a group of small children wearing their smocked party frocks.

As young ladies at school we were taught the art of embroidery. Table cloths, tray cloths, antimacassars, table runners, place mats and dressing-table sets, nothing escaped our eager needles. Chain stitch, daisy stitch, knot stitch, blanket stitch — the options were many, and the linen table cloths with their blue transfer patterns waiting to be embroidered with the rainbow colours of Anchor's silk threads were enticing.

Of all the handicrafts, I suspect that as a nation we are best known for our knitting. A pair of needles and a ball of wool are all that is needed to create something beautiful and highly satisfying. Each coastal area of Britain developed over time its own regional knitting pattern, and any fisherman could tell at a glance where another came from by the stitches on his navy-blue guernsey which the fishermen still wear today. They were originally worked in very thick yarn on very fine needles, making them wind and weatherproof. The cream knitting of the Aran Isles is instantly recognizable by its bobble stitches and richly encrusted texture, and the Shetland Islands are well known for their Fair Isle. When my son James was born I was given a beautiful pram cover with the symbols for health and happiness for a new-born son knitted into the pattern. When we were children our mother always made us Fair Isle jumpers, with bands of colour done in stocking stitch on a plain background, and matching berets and mittens often found their way into our Christmas stockings. She is now over eighty years of age and never sits down without some knitting in her hands. The moment there is a new baby in the family the old knitting patterns come out, and the tiny wrapover vests she made for my newborn babies were so small that they have kept their dolls warm ever since. We were quite small when we were taught to knit squares to be made into blankets for the army. However, I never did graduate to three needles, unlike my mother, whom I can remember knitting socks for His Majesty's soldiers.

The Toybox

WHEN the children ask me to play a game with them and we look in the toybox in the nursery, I get a pleasant sense of familiarity. Many of the toys and games are the ones I enjoyed when I was a child. A box of bricks will keep a small child engaged for hours, building castles and knocking them down, and my daughter loved to turn picture bricks over and over until she had completed the image of Snow White or Cinderella. While snakes and ladders is a vicious board game in which one can unashamedly gloat over the misfortunes of others, and which depends entirely on luck, many games are instructive as well as being fun. I can well remember playing Woodland Happy Families when I was a little girl and having the rules of politeness firmly instilled. We always had to say 'please' when asking for a card, and 'thank you' on receiving it. As children we particularly liked Pepys Happy Families cards drawn originally in 1851, with Miss Bun, the Baker's Daughter, and Master Soot, the Sweep's Son. Draughts and chess teach us cunning and diplomacy and to anticipate the actions of others, while patience and solitaire are important in that we learn to amuse ourselves.

When I was quite small, my grandmother gave me a small leather case containing two miniature packs of patience cards, and taught me clock patience. It has to be the most irritating game I know for the likelihood of it coming out is slim,

but the satisfaction when it does is enormous. Monopoly and Cluedo are great favourites, but can go on for hours, so we tend to reserve them for holidays, when time is of no importance. I remember when Scrabble was invented and the pleasure of the grown-ups when they realized that finally here was a game which was good for our spelling. Chinese Chequers is a splendid game, and I remember once crossing an airport with the board in my hand as we had landed at a vital moment in the game. Some of the best games are the simplest: all you need for Cats Cradle is a length of string, and for a game of hopscotch just a piece of chalk with which to draw it.

I am particularly partial to jigsaw puzzles, and at all levels. I love the ones for very tiny children, with knobs on the wooden pieces so that they can push them into the holes. I loved to see my children doing the floor puzzle of the big red London bus or watch their delight as they pieced together their favourite characters from their picture books. Over the past few years we have created everything from dinosaurs, fairy glades and Degas ballerinas to a giant wooden map of the world. Doing a jigsaw puzzle is my own private remedy for stress. If I bring home the strain of city life, I find that sitting down with a puzzle and applying my wits to something so different instantly changes my mood.

Winter Activities

IN England we expect to have snow at some point, even in a mild winter, yet when we awaken to a white world we are surprised and never really prepared. There is nothing that excites children more than the first snow, and they rush through their breakfast in order to be the first to go outside and break the clean, even surface. Through the windows we can see their breath as they throw snowballs at each other and play around in the snow. Later we may help them to build snowmen, borrowing a cap and scarf and using twigs for the face and buttons. When I was a child, skiing was a sport only performed abroad, but tobogganing was a favourite pastime, and those without sledges slid down the bumpy fields on tin trays.

I have always been fascinated by Victorian Christmas cards showing wonderful scenes of whole families ice-skating in St James's Park. Ladies in long velvet dresses and fur muffs holding the hands of small children and gentlemen in top hats and cloaks. I think it has only snowed in England on Christmas Day about half a dozen times this century, and in my memory it has rarely been possible to ice-skate; perhaps the winters are milder than they used to be, or else the Victorian painters gave themselves a lot of licence. Charles Dickens wrote of skating parties in *Pickwick Papers*, however, and his account of Mr Pickwick on the ice is a masterpiece. Taking a walk one snowy day in Kensington Gardens with the children to see the statue of Peter Pan, I remember being amazed at seeing people swimming in the Serpentine. In the country, particularly in hilly areas like the Yorkshire Moors, a fall of snow often has very serious consequences, for it can mean buried sheep and isolated farmhouses. After the first snowfall the snowplough comes out, and grit and salt are put down to clear the roads. When I was a child, and we were living in Heptonstall on the edge of the Moors, we were once snowed up for six weeks. Yorkshire housewives prepare for such an eventuality by keeping a well-stocked store cupboard and larder.

Theatre Life

URING the Christmas holidays we were always taken as children to the Grand Theatre in Leeds or the Alhambra in Bradford 'to see a show'. Sometimes this was classical ballet, such as *The Nutcracker* or *Coppelia*, danced by one of the great London companies. Another time it was *Iolanthe*, and we enjoyed the witty lyrics of W. S. Gilbert accompanied by the music of Sir Arthur Sullivan

The 1950s were a great time for musicals, and *Annie Get Your Gun*, *Showboat* and *Carousel* were all part of my education. So indeed were the operettas of Ivor Novello, and my father told us how, when he had seen *Perchance to Dream*, the great man himself walked sideways down the stairs to show his famous profile. Burlesque and music hall were still popular, but were considered unsuitable for us children, and I had to wait to see Laurence Olivier give his great performance in *The Entertainer* in London years later. Olivier took the part of a one-time music-hall entertainer, eeking out a living in seaside summer shows in late 1950s Britain. On my first visit to London, aged seven, we went to see The Crazy Gang at the Victoria Palace, where Nervo and Knox dressed up as babies in prams and the inimitable Tony Hancock, who was on the same bill, entertained us with his self-deprecating humour.

Quite the best holiday treat, however, was the pantomime. An eccentric English institution, it takes stories from fairy tales, characters from the Italian *commedia dell' arte*, and adds ballet, magic, juggling, slapstick and lots of audience participation. The principal boy is usually played by a girl, and the older woman or Dame, be it Mother Goose or the wicked stepmother, by a man in drag. While the scene is being set for the grand finale when the prince and princess come down the marble staircase, the Dame is in front of the curtain teaching us a song written on a big screen, and encouraging some of the children on to the stage with him. James and Charlotte Rose love to go backstage to see the outrageous costumes and theatrical props in the Dame's dressing-room, but the funniest moment of their lives came last year when the Dame came out into the audience at the end of the kitchen scene, and tipped a plate of meringue all over their father's head.

Christmas

AT the beginning of December, the children start to open their Advent Calendars, eagerly searching for the tiny numbered windows they will open each day until Christmas Eve. I well remember the joy of finding all the symbols of Christmas there. This is the time to start thinking too about Christmas cards, which should theoretically be sent on 6 December, the Feast of St Nicholas — but seldom are. We were always encouraged as children to make our own cards, and after the end of the school term the cold days of December were spent colouring, cutting and glueing. I think this was when I learned that a present that I had made myself was appreciated much more than one that had been bought.

At the end of the Michaelmas term the schools perform nativity plays, For me, several decades of hearing the words 'And it came to pass, in those days …' have only increased the magic. Little children dressed up with large paper wings as angels, or in long woollen robes as shepherds, are invariably a touching sight. Other schools hold a carol service where the carols are sung in small piping voices accompanied by the recorder or the triangle, and the lessons read by the older children give a pattern to the service. The children process down the aisle and take their place in the tableau, and after a short address by the vicar, the organ plays the refrain from 'O Come all ye faithful' and all join in. The tunes and the words, familiar from years of repetition, unite the whole congregation in a feeling of goodwill.

One of the things that makes Christmas special is the decoration of the house. By bringing the forest into the home, as in medieval times, we transform our surroundings, and branches of fir, holly and ivy all add to a festive atmosphere. Of prime importance is the Christmas tree, always real, which we are careful to plant out again later if it has retained its roots.

The custom of having a Christmas tree at home was introduced to England by Prince Albert after his marriage to Queen Victoria. Originally Christmas trees were decorated with dried fruit, nuts and bonbons. When I was small we had a selection of glass ornaments: birds which clipped on to the branches with their feet and balanced with small bristly tails; coloured glass balls, and long crystal drops like part of a chandelier — all set off against strands of multi-coloured fairy lights. I personally love an abundant tree, with presents surrounding the base, and although it is fashionable nowadays to have a themed tree in one colour, I would never be able to achieve this. The children come home from school with tinsel and decorations they have made, and it would be a hard-hearted mother who refused to put them on. Christmas is a time for children, and I think it is important that they should be allowed to make their contribution. Since they were quite small, our children have helped me put the holly on the window-sills and make a wreath for the front door.

Carols should strictly only be sung after Advent ends on Christmas Day, but these days we are more relaxed about when to begin. The tradition of itinerant carol singing began in the reign of Queen Elizabeth I, when

carol singers were banned from Church premises for being unruly, and were obliged to wander through the villages instead. As a result carol singers may often be found on Christmas Eve and earlier, their lanterns lighting their hymn sheets, going from house to house. In small country hamlets they are invited into the hall of the Manor House, where the house party will have assembled and where the host will be serving hot and spicy mulled wine.

Many people prefer to go to Midnight Mass on Christmas Eve rather than Matins on Christmas morning. As a nation we are not as dutiful as we once were about our church-going, and it is wonderful to sing the time-honoured lines in a church packed with worshippers. Coming out into the cold night air afterwards, going home and hanging the stockings is always an enchanted time for me, anticipating the pleasure the children will have when they wake up in the morning and find them. We fill their stockings with tiny presents together with tangerines, nuts and fruit in the Victorian way, and then leave a mince pie and a glass of sherry for Father Christmas on the mantelpiece. Many is the time I tried as a child to stay awake in order to see him come down the chimney to eat it.

A Christmas Feast

OST households with children awake early on Christmas Day. In our household we breakfast early on cold roast York ham and toast, then after church we exchange presents, sitting around the tree listening to Carols from Kings College, Cambridge. At midday other members of the family start to arrive, and the festivities start with a glass of champagne and what is known in Yorkshire as a 'biting on', a little smoked salmon on brown bread to keep us going. This is a trying time for the cook, for whether turkey, goose or duck is being served, the lunch is a challenge to prepare. Our meal consists of the bird, together with small sausages, sprouts, parsnips, carrots and roast potatoes, served with bread sauce, cranberry jelly and chestnut stuffing. Meanwhile the Christmas pudding will have been steaming away for the past hour. When the time is right, brandy is poured over the pudding, a sprig of holly is put in the top, and it is set alight, to general glee, before being eaten with a sweet white sauce or brandy butter. Even now the meal is far from over, for the table is once again covered with seasonal food. Mince pies, piled in a silver basket, are served, and a half stilton wrapped in damask is served with celery. At this point a decanter of port is put on the table, a drink even those suffering from gout can hardly resist. Baskets of fresh walnuts, hazelnuts, and brazil nuts are passed around, and the children try to master the giant nutcrackers; boxes of dates and dried figs are opened, and only when the last cracker has been pulled and the Queen is about to make her Christmas Day broadcast to the nation and the Commonwealth do we leave the table.

The rest of Christmas Day is spent playing games, from charades to card games and consequences, and on displays of dancing and reciting. At tea-time a Christmas cake is served. This is a rich fruit cake covered in marzipan and crisp white icing and decorated with the figures of Father Christmas and the snowman which are brought out year after year. On Boxing Day, we like to venture outside and go for a good walk, then settle in with a log fire and a new book and even start to write thank you letters. Cold cuts of turkey and ham are served, and it is a day of relaxation and recovery. We each have our own way of celebrating New Year's Eve, for this is the time when we put the old year to bed and make our resolutions for the year to come. Our tradition is to welcome in the New Year by partying with friends; at midnight we join hands and sing the Scottish air Auld Lang Syne to the chimes of Big Ben. It is all part of the familiar ritual of The Christmas Season, and each year we agree that we would not have it any other way.

I WOULD like to thank Colin Webb and all at Pavilion Books for their support and encouragement, not to mention patience. Rachel King oversaw the project, Steve Dobell was my editor, and Bernard Higton created yet another beautiful design. Having worked so happily with Rosemary Weller for Penhaligon's, I knew I could entrust her to interpret my ideas visually. It has been a pleasure to work with such a harmonious team. I would also like to acknowledge my gratitude to the staff of the London Library who courteously and patiently answered my enquiries and referred me to the appropriate books. While browsing there one day I discovered *The Book of Days*, edited by R. Chambers in 1862, in which I found details of many of the traditions that interested me. Godfrey Smith's comprehensive book *The English Season* gave me the information I needed for certain events. My mother's bulging old purple recipe book was consulted on more than one occasion and I would like to thank my sister, Susan Newman, for checking the recipes for me. My friends Anthea Proud and Paula Rigby, both fine upholders of English traditions, lent me their books and Anthea allowed me to photograph her Dorset smock and embroidery. David Sweetman was an excellent source of literary information and Nicholas Pneumaticatos was my authority on protocol. Finally, I would like to thank my husband, David Rainer, for keeping the family running while I wrote the book, and for providing me at the same time with the technology to deliver the book on disc.